When This World Comes to an End

When This World Comes to an End

✳

KATE CAYLEY

BRICK BOOKS

Library and Archives Canada Cataloguing in Publication

Cayley, Kate
    When this world comes to an énd / Kate Cayley.

Poems.
ISBN 978-1-926829-83-8

    I. Title.

PS8605.A945W44 2013   C811'.6   C2013-900059-3

We acknowledge the Canada Council for the Arts, the Government of Canada through the Canada Book Fund, and the Ontario Arts Council for their support of our publishing program.

The author photo was taken by Carmen Farrell.

This book is set in Minion Pro, designed by Robert Slimbach and released by Adobe Systems in 1990.

The cover image is "Diving horse, 1908" from the William James collection, City of Toronto Archives, Fonds 1244, Item 191.

Design and layout by Cheryl Dipede.
Printed and bound by Sunville Printco Inc.

Brick Books
431 Boler Road, Box 20081
London, Ontario N6K 4G6
www.brickbooks.ca

For Dan DeMatteis

"There is a light in the darkness and the darkness has never quenched it"

CONTENTS

SIGNS AND WONDERS

Oh there'll be signs and wonders
Oh there'll be signs and wonders
Yes there'll be signs and wonders
When this world comes to an end

—folk song, Appalachian Mountains

BOOK OF DAYS

*

Zola, Bravest of Leonardo's Apprentices, Leaps from the Tower of San Francesco Wearing His Master's Wings

At night, my master dreams time and heaven.
I, his apprentice, dream nothing.

I am the mirror that gives him back, the sigh
breathed into his mouth at night, youth
that saves him from his age.
I am salvation. The angel beating
copper wings.

My body, strong as woven reeds, built
to remember his body when it is dust.
A splinter of memory lodged
under my heart, my shoulder blades, where now
the wings sprout madly, tied with silk, the harness
casing my skin, woven chrysalis. I leaped, I flew.

There was a moment of lift. I thought
I could veer left or right, soar between spires
past the reds and blues of cathedral windows, leave
the cracked ground. Leave him,
an old glitter-eyed man who imagines
luridly, carnally, all he cannot do himself.

Then I fell. Clutching at time, I went down.
A crunch of bones,
stone. Earth had the last word.

I did not die. He held my head, he prayed
for me, I sucked my life back
through his mouth,
his sigh saved me for my age.

Now we are even.

Persephone

She partitioned each
red seed with a swift tongue.

She knew what he was offering—
the earth beneath the earth, his troubled self,
forceful, unmade, a blank and stubborn face,
his mouth twitching like a child
since he had not known, before her, what it was he wanted.
He had no cunning
and this won her, with the wish
for silence and the restful dark.

                    Some women desire winter
more than summer, ends more than beginnings,
each seed disappearing down her throat.

The Later Auden

In the evening, wine, then vodka. Auden, grievously mathematical,
lays his head down at the end of each apportioned day. The guests
must be gone by nine thirty. Timetabled, ticking off
the flyblown minutes, he gets hungry
only when the clock strikes the appropriate hour, lonely
only between nightfall and morning. Wrists shaking,
fingers yellow stained, he sucks his cuffs, murmurs madly
that all things are roads, that God is a comfort, that he should
have been a desiccated bishop eyeing the choir.

His voice dies out in the muffled cloth. Reed-bent
but hopeful, he encounters each day's white wasteland.
The pen strikes through, mapping the way
to an enduring solitude, age-dimmed. Wine for speech,
vodka for oblivion, he rifles through the spattered sheets, reflecting that
language still fails when faced

with such an ending. Putting this down
to faults of construction, he prepares for bed. Lies in the dark, his hair
thatching for an unsheltered head, muttering,
suspicious, watchful of all human love.

William Kemmler Remembering his Wife

*William Kemmler was the first man to die in the electric chair,
having murdered his wife Tillie with a hatchet in 1889.*

I was not a *good husband.*
Whiskey lay like piss in dozens of glasses,
I pissed holes in the floor, drowned the mice.
I tore through our small life,
streaked like lightning, my blood
boiled down thick, my eyelids
permanently swollen. She sidestepped me
whenever she could. I studied
her hair, coiled and frowzy with light,
the sweat beading on her upper lip. The first blow
I though she'd fall apart easily as
a jug breaking, streaming water.

Seventeen cuts, her skull sharded, a map
of red drops on the wall.

Some country I have never been.

Do you understand me?
I stood back, the continents shifted, the new country
raised up on the kitchen wall, I saw it.

I do not avoid death, not since.
We have passed each other, nodding, he knows
I am his twin, his face in the mirror.
I straighten my cuffs.

Everything there is to fear I have already seen.

6

Reading Gwendolyn MacEwen's T. E. Lawrence poems

When I was a child, my great-grandmother's *Lives of the Saints*
rested on a high shelf, dusty, mouldered, back cover missing.

It meant: the past is a foreign city.

The book said that a particular saint "gave away

the world," as though the world could be given and got, a jewel
tossed under the passing feet of Christ. I did not know

the world could be *given*. A sudden flight
from a motorcycle, an arc to rival the sky,

the unexpected sound of broken bones.
Martyrs, willing to exist as an idea—

the word and not the flesh. A woman is writing in a room:
words are a line that bleed her dry, and he, overdrawn hero, also bleeds

her, and bleeds himself, his breath stopped by
the cold rain, a roaring heaven, a quick turn of the road.

Giving the world away, they did not ask or know
if kindness or goodness would come of it.

Is that the life of a saint? A perfection of abdication, giving
away ordinary sweetness for a truth, which gives

without knowing purpose or end. The gamblers of the world,
that woman, that man, daring to believe that

the body falls in perfect grace, redeemed,
the risk worth taking:

if one must die for something,
there's nothing like a cross
from which to contemplate the world.

Charles Dodgson Looking at Alice Liddell

Today, a young man
sees teacups and cards as possible first principles,
wonders about queens, croquet and language,
invents new kinds of butterflies, adjusts

his collar in the mirror.

She is not golden, nor does she pout—
wary of cameras and inventive minds,
self-consciously ragged in a Victorian study
under that artificial sexless eye, or

leaning out of a boat in July,
smiling blithely and pretending it isn't raining.

Her veins are blue as the small snakes
from which he shies, her teeth
thin flakes pickaxed from white rock.

He does not look at her mouth.

She is suspicious of guile, so
he pauses, stricken
by painful, stainless, unaffected love,
sincere as childhood, and as remote.

The camera pleads his case,
a silent chaperone, an entryway
and sanctuary too, from time and place,
keeping her with him always

safe and dry, away
from the riff-raff and banal
expressions of the everyday.

A gaze so plain
that she will love him even when
the sentimental haze fades
and he is left

lonesome and boring, an old lecturer
in spotless clothes.

Today though, he is
with her,
fortified from time—

this machine, this mirror
through which a past is never past, and all
you were, will always be—

if only in a desk drawer, for the tentative eyes
and prayerful dreams of melancholy men.

The Later Life of Judas Iscariot

Traditionally red-haired, he stands out in a crowd.
Orange-ginger grizzle going grey, freckles on fish-white
puckered skin, a sleepless, constipated look.
I wonder though if this is anything but
the theatrics of wives' tales—the birthmark, the portent
and, for ease of identification, a villain's swivelling eye.

In fact, he is unremarkable, pleasant.
Good at parties, capable with money,
knows a thing or two about wine, well-read
without embarrassing learnedness, well-
invested, a patron of various charities, kindly
in that purely personal way. Retired, he bought
a small house with a Japanese rock garden, and collected
pictures, and was happy. It was only
the other apostles who wished he'd hanged himself
in that ravening field planted with silver pieces, the rope
pulling his face purple, his eyes
staring at the sun. Dante

saw him in the mouth of the beast, but who can say?
He saw only the backside, it could have been
anyone, and Dante was
a confused and trembling witness.

These days he sits in a deck chair, watching the water,
his face lined and friendly. No complaints,
no mark on the neck.

Simone Weil

Cigarette in yellowing hand
she is wreathed in smoke,
a saint hoping to burn.
Her free hand
wanders, fingering

a pen, stale bread;
eyes restless,
knowing truth is silent
and God absent,
yet,
like thought, they hover
on the outside of certainties.

She shifts a little,
picks up the pen

and waits
as saints do,
in perfect solitude.

Walking

She is light now.

He carries her
soft like hair, bride-soft, down
the new path. His eyes are wide
and stretched open.

With only a little life left, he is
a tourist in his own country:
surprised by landscape,
conscious of history.

Perhaps he thought:
is this her true weight? Was she ever
any heavier than this?

When her eyes had lids
and her tongue was wet
and her hands darkened in the sun
like ordinary hands.

Neanderthal Man, Theory and Practice

The world is not ending, let us say this.
It has ended.

German miners, 1856—picking at the limestone,
burrowing in the creases of the earth—found
the flattened skulls, cracked thighs,
long fingers, disjointed arms clawing out
of that darkness.

These creatures buried their dead, ground stone,
they spoke, their hands tore at the roots of trees. Perhaps
they cared for the lame, the blind, led them
over the rougher earth. They may have chewed
the food of the old, fed them tenderly
through thickets of rotted teeth.

They also ate their dead, the flesh ripped
away from the bone, sinews white, red wet hands.

The miners feared the bones. But one man, young,
hacking his life away, held
a skull in his hands, the eye sockets
addressing his own eyes.

Then he put it down and cracked it with his pick.
The other men looked away, but did not protest:
a long hard day, little time.

Nick Drake and Emily Dickinson Meet in the Afterlife

They are cautious virgins, and unfriendly
as they have always been.

These two never loved the flesh, so death
is already peculiarly their own. Breathless
they look each other up and down—
her eyes that famous residual sherry,
his blank as stones on the riverbed.

They both wear white now, though she always has.
They feel awkward in their wings, find
the light brighter than they wished, unfettered consciousness
a terror for those whose art was limit.

This is to say they recognize each other. Neither
expected this. The end, they thought,
would mean a sealed box, a final solitude,
the heart intact as an egg, forever.

He tells her about the thin grey light
when the songs came, halting, in pieces,
and she tells him about her furtive sleep,
and a thousand poems hidden in a drawer.

A Journey by Train

When a man leaves a place, he takes a train. Sometimes he is obliged to
stand. If he is able, he brings a suitcase, a walking stick and a shiny hat.
These are the images of dreams, old films, photographs. He thinks: I will
be a traveller, I will leave my town. When the angel of death comes to my
door, he will be told I have already left. When he pursues me down the road,
he will not recognize me in my new suit. When I come to the city, it will be
brighter, and better organized, full of street corners where a man may fade
into ochre-lit walls, and I will vanish. He will never find me again.

CURIO: TWELVE PHOTOGRAPHS

✳

Daguerre Photographs Paris, 1838

Louis-Jacques-Mandé Daguerre (1787-1851) was an artist and chemist who invented
the Daguerreotype process of photography. His most famous photograph, taken in
1838 or 1839, shows a Paris street. While the street was full of people, exposure time
was so long (over ten minutes) that the street appears empty except for a man having
his boots polished by a young boy. "Boulevard du Temple" is the first photograph to
show a person.

I

The wind arcs
down the column of his spine
from where
the collar stands up stiff, the hair
rises on the back of his neck.

His nails are dirty, the cuticles bleeding.

From his perch on the hill he sees
storefronts, figures
heaving in and out of sight, scuttling
through the dust and the stone—
cockroaches pinned by daylight.

Standing, he adjusts the lens.

A boy polishes
an old man's shoes, his quick hand
thickened by distance, arm raised as if
staving off a blow.

Daguerre aims the camera at the dirty street,
his lens the eye without vision, the choice
which cannot choose, blind finger of light,
salvation of time.

II

Even the houses look like ghosts now.

The darkroom reveals
an absence, the expected
disappointment:

noon, but the street is empty.
Windows and doors wide as question marks,
the city distilled and freed of people—

but wait,
he tightens his silver-stained fingers—

there in the corner, two figures are safe,
the preserved perpetual husk of what is gone.

The old man stoops, the boy
polishes his shoes, quick hand thickened
by distance, arm raised as if
staving off a blow.

A Wedding Teacup, Toronto, 1907

A life does not consist of objects,
but perhaps objects are its only
certain evidence.

In china, as in flesh, frailty
is sometimes evidence of fortitude.

The wife knew this, her veins
sickly as winter spiders,
the cup on the table a thread
joining her to her mother's house, reminder
that whatever happens, certain hours
remain the same.

A life does not consist of objects,
but the cup looks round as the world,
stares like time's one good eye.

Halifax Flea Market: Two Photographs

1. Fishing Boat and Two Men Facing Away, 1912

An odd angle,
as if the camera had tilted.

The rigging yellowish, the jumbled deck
sepia with patches of white—
life preservers, or maybe
baskets for fish.

Written in a straight hand
against the slope of the boat:

setting trawl
        "Venosta"

The two men huddled
side by side aboard the Venosta,
the faded photograph suddenly
like sunlight, an early morning.

The men's legs have almost disappeared
so you can't see whether
they're sitting together, backs to the camera,
or walking away unaware.

But if you peer hard into the background, you'll find
two other figures facing towards you,
one staring affably, one smiling,
both too small to really be seen.

One holds a coil of rope,
one a life preserver waving
at a big white sky.

2. Kisses Implied by Postscript, 1905

Rows of unsmiling ladies and gentlemen,
a class or Society. Ladies in white,
gentlemen in black but for white collars.

One woman has a mandolin, one wears a hat
off to one side and looks embarrassed. The rest
run together, polite, meek or wistful faces
against the brick wall and warehouse doors.
The picture's back is dark with age, ink lightening
in a round thin hand:

what do you
think of this
I expect you
can recognize
Beattie. I will
send you one
of myself when
Walter takes it
Love to all

       Beattie

a line driven under it, and three Xs.

No way to see
where Beattie is,
but someone has dipped their finger
in ink and carefully
printed over one woman's face,
fingerprint black against white
in furtive love or hate.

Married Couple with Baby, 1910

Cracked teacup, gnarled thread, a child
tangling her new wool.

The drawing room sofa
full of headaches and old bones.

A practiced eye, the camera knew
what dull unhappiness a brighter light
might yet reveal.

Still, he loves her best.

The baby, stirring, blurs and breaks
the lines of its own face
as if returning to air,

escaping its mother's tight
hold, its father's eye.

The White Horse Divers, Lake Ontario, 1908

Twice a day, two white horses
climb a scaffold, pause
and dive down a long way, then clamber
out again, dripping.

Was he aware of the crowd's long gasp? Did she,
feeling the stream of air, the startle of water
have a complacent moment, knowing herself
Pegasus, though without wings?

Or was the plunge
each afternoon and evening mirrored
by a lurch in the curve of the belly, no matter
how many times they climbed that scaffold
for the great fall, the sun, the reverse birth

as the lake closed over them? Then the panic
and struggle toward shore, applause,
blankets and a brief respite, just long enough
to forget the seething people, the rickety planks,
the sleek tumble down.

J. W. GORMAN'S
DIVING HORSES
THE WHITE BEAUTIES
KING AND QUEEN
Dive Here Every
Afternoon and Evening

The slender scaffold bridges out
over the lake, the horse
halfway through a tense and sunlit dive,
its freakish grace transfiguring
the crowd, a trickle of the mildly curious.

Close your eyes.

There you are, flattened
to that breath-stealing
photograph; you are absorbed, a presence
in white. But are you the horse

or a woman in the crowd below,
white dress streaked
with grey, suddenly, painfully weeping
for the flight before you?

Or perhaps
you are the more dangerous, more beautiful
tragedy, the circular motion
of afternoon and evening, the king and queen
trembling before each execution, then delivered
from the water, given food, love
from a silent man who brushes their coats.

Be the horse. Be patient and simple, blind
to anything beyond this moment, step out
on trembling legs toward the lake, knowing that
there is something behind this, something
that sustains, propels, repeats.

White Horse Diver #2

Where in unconsciousness do horses lodge?
The grief and splendour, the panic's eye
hovering in the doorway of waking?
The modest sadness of the horse,
banished from roads and fields, nudges in
unasked. The people lined below
the improbable scaffold, gawking
at the grace of a moment's fall, this
lithe diver stretching above an answer
to a dream suppressed, a longing
for nights of hooves and sky. Tenderness heaves
upwards from tight throats, the crowd
awestruck by this whitest creature's flight.
Then the sigh exhaled, the ripples in its wake.

Girl in a Checked Dress on a Slum Doorstep, 1912

Yes, she sits here every day.
Yes, she answers quickly when you speak.
Yes, she just got it recently, was diffident.
Yes, her mother told her to tie up rags to soak it up.

No, I think it is not her baby. I do not know
if it is the neighbour's baby, her mother's baby
or her niece or nephew. Don't know if she helps out
regularly or if someone thrust it
at her, *here, I'll be back soon,*
and left her sitting there, capably balancing
those starfish limbs.

Yes, she has shoes, but she does not
often wear them, why get them dirty when feet
stain far less easily, are easier to repair
when crushed or torn by stones, glass or wheels?
Yes, she is pleased to have the man take her picture.
No, no-one has taken her picture
before this morning, but it has not troubled her.

Yes, I kept turning back
to this photograph, her fingers
clutching the blanket tightly, as if
the small wind will tear it away.

Painter in Her Studio, 1907

Behind her head, a print from Japan.
Thin strokes in an age of heaviness, light
among these dark expensive furnishings.

She is white haired,
the pallet held—cautious—
over the landscape of her dress.

Now colour
can only be guessed at,
a drainage of significance
simplifying her eyes,
black and grey vanishing to white.

A bare floor. A worn rug.

A woman who has reluctantly
put longing aside, lives
in the time of last things.

A print from Japan.

Perhaps she sighed
for such imagined austerity, that sweep of line
cutting open all sight, rendering the world

sparse and proportionate, a beauty of absences.

Perhaps when alone (which is often) she dreams
of a clean white world, sliced with black and red,
where she has never been,

and a delicate, different snow.

Ballerina on a Horse, Midway, 1915

Something in common with soldiers, she.
Whether or not she screwed them in the tent, she knows
the value of practice, poise, a straight leg, a cynical eye.

Stoutish lady clutching at girlhood, pointed toes, tight ribbons,
selling hard a face of chalk and honey. Her kohl-rimmed eyes look
punched by an expert small fist. Mouth red and stiff

as the furrows and mounds of her manufactured hair. Poof
of feathers—time for a little furtive dusting—one arm
held over her head, as she's seen

creditable dancers do. The other hand
holds the small sweet whip, more for a wink
to nervous watching men than for this sturdy horse

bulged with failure and age. Veined and pasted white,
as if her face, his hide endured the same touch-ups, afternoon
and evening. Rhinestones on the bridle. This pony

no cousin of the white horse divers, no magnificence
of falling. Just the swish
and sigh of synonymous days.

Together they are the dream of women and horses
boiled down to a lumpen shimmer of flesh.
Both bear the same dark eyes, stoic, turned away.

Blind Twins Facing Away From Each Other, 1850

When we were children, our father
gave me a chestnut. And her, lace.

This was to make us know
the differences in the world.
What is made, yields.
What is grown, stands.
It endures, it refuses. We stand
together, blindness our single property.
I honour
the differences between us.

Many lacemakers are blind, he said,
(a simple, avaricious man)
and their fingers know
the knots, the thread, better
than eyes do.

                    He touched
my eyelids, blessed me. Then, hers.
Though that I only guess.

Her hands wither, her hair falling
athwart my face at night, the only
touch I know, bound together
in permanent twilight, fingers laced.

Silver Cross Mother, 1919

She rides a cart,
medal on brown coat, small hat on head;
she mocks the crowd, waving.

Memory. Loss. She is both, she will
harbour both under her ribs, excavate
whatever else was there. A tight hermetic grief
too close for sunlight to slide through, too spare
for narrative cleverness, a quiet seepage,
as if under her dress
her breasts leaked blood.

Beside her,
waving flags,
some small serious children
who are not hers.

Considering Photographs

Here is the oldest person you will ever know,
stretching through all your callow years.
Shadowing the small locked doors, recesses
of memory reach down toward the youngest known.

Stretching through all your callow years
the presence of the eldest, whatever they have told you
of their memory, reaches down toward the youngest known
by you, you pass this age to childhood, and on.

The presence of the eldest, whatever they have told you is
reimagined through your life, given to other ears
by you. You pass this age to childhood, and on.
This is not history, it is time itself, spoken.

Reimagined through your life, given to other ears,
this is the only recourse to particular past. You know
this is not history, it is time itself, spoken.
The speechless photograph gives voice: the dead speak here.

This is the only recourse to a particular past, you know.
Shadowing the small locked doors, recesses
the speechless photograph gives voice to: the dead speak here.
Here is the oldest person you will ever know.

SIGNS AND WONDERS

*

Light of Another Sun

That was the summer when all the bees died, and the water turned yellow. I thought about you that summer. I am spending quite a bit of time alone, with both the girls at school all day, and Tim and I never talked much after you went away. When I remember you we are in a garden, and the bees are buzzing. Karen came to me one day from the backyard to show me handfuls of little lifeless bees, soft as her breath, brittle as her bones. Even her pockets were full of them. They spilled out onto the floor, which we recently had redone in terracotta tiles. She lined a glass bowl with moss and kept them as pets, until Nancy ate one and I just had to throw them away. Then when the water turned yellow overnight and the radio and the internet said everything was fine, we are dealing with it, we are trained in emergency preparedness, Nancy got a strange growth behind her ear and Tim complained that there was a bitter taste in his mouth, like burnt coffee. So we started sleeping in the basement because it seemed safer, and we turned on the radio and on the radio it said that someone had reported there was another earth, another planet, and it seemed that on this other earth there was water. And I looked at our water, and the tap dripped yellow and then stopped. And I thought of this empty planet, somewhere, elsewhere, and I find myself more and more thinking of it, and of you there, drinking that water, looking into the light of another sun.

Love Poem from the Dictionary

Night

the period of darkness between
one day and the next

nightfall
*(we shall not reach home
before night)*

the darkness of the night
(as black as night)

a night or evening appointed
for some activity
or spent
or regarded
in a certain way
(last night was a great night out)

or the musty red-eyed
wishful frustrated world
suddenly caught and
perfect in this
what is it
this
what is it
this what moment is it
a palpitation a shivering
stretching away stretching into

Absence

the state of being
away from a place
or person
the time or duration of being away
lack

the condition of uncertainty the pause
thoughtful
before a kiss

Clothes

garments worn to cover
the body
and limbs

bedclothes

and sometimes both discarded
trifling away the dark

Skin

the flexible continuous
covering of a human body

the skin of a flayed animal
with or
without hair

an outer layer
or covering

a film like a skin
on the surface of a liquid

the planking or
plating of a ship or boat

inside or outside the ribs

to become covered with new skin

Time

the indefinite continued progress
of existence
events etc
in past present and future
regarded as
a whole
the progress of this
as affecting
persons or things
*(stood the test
of time)*

in full "Father Time"
the personification of time
especially an old
man bald
but with a forelock
carrying a scythe
and hourglass

a portion of time
(the time of the plague
prehistoric time
the scientists of the time)

a measurable portion of time
the period of time at one's disposal
(am wasting my time
had no time
how much time do you
need)

a point of time
in hours and minutes

(what time is it you say rolling over out of sight
of the clock hair flying into your eyes

or what is the time)

or an occasion
(last time I saw you)

(but when was that)
how much time do we have

a lifetime
(will last my time)

but then shaking herself she went

downstairs where there was water
food light from the street
and the relieved silence as if she

had never been there at all
and even the bed will not say
yes or no
now

(and what time is it)

Absolve

often followed by "from" or "of"
set or pronounce free
from blame or obligation etc

acquit
pronounce not guilty

pardon or give absolution

and in this case also
leaving ending division

and other possible conclusions
to a kiss or several

a night or several

even a year or several
times in which
words were webs and skin better
somewhat than words

(is skin ever really better than words?)

Grimm in the Black Forest

In fairy tales, a woman is often sought, though sometimes
the seeker. Nothing happens inside. It is all marked
on the skin, for everyone to see—the pained
feet, singed hair, terrible silence.

The woman serves and waits
with troubling love,
learning patience from desire.

She goes
to churchyards, her flesh sick with fear,
to make nettle shirts, stinging her hands
to blisters and welts.

She serves the blacksmith, a man
who's never heard one word of consolation.
For seven years, she will melt herself
down and climb
a mountain of glass,

a mess and muddle of light, each piece
embedded in her body—she shines
as she faces the wedded end
with nothing to say.

Three Cautions for Water

1. Homeward

On Tuesday it rained so much that when the girl came home, her mother
had been eaten by a school of fish.

The girl knew this because her mother always wore a pink arm band on
her left arm. When the girl paddled into her front yard she saw it caught
in the lowest tree branch. It was savaged by the very small teeth of very
small fish. The girl identified these marks correctly because she was a
resourceful child, who carried a jeweller's eyeglass in her pocket. She had
paddled home in the janitor's slop pail; she paddled with a shovel and used
the janitor's jacket as a sail. She had managed all this without sullying her
white shoes.

When she saw the arm band she exclaimed O dolourous day! O woeful
chance! and clammered and yammered shamefully, spinning round
and round in the weeds. Her hair flew up in lightning streaks, her teeth
ground black pepper, her tears were pearl white with lamentation. She
smashed her face down into the water. Then she wiped her eyes and made
herself a stiff one, going round and round in the tepid water. It's not so
bad. It could be worse. She had another. She began to feel festive. She
roosted on the chimney.

In the morning it was sunny. A pigeon had died in the chimney. She had
breakfast. She turned round three times and tore the shingles with her
scrabbled red hands. In time, she made a hole and crawled into the house.
The water had receded from the upper floor. She danced a jig, her feet
tap-tapping and squelching on the rotting boards. She danced so fast she
gave off sparks and black smoke. The heat dried up all the water from her
house.

The girl caroused and revelled all by herself. The neighbours barely
noticed her.

Years passed.

When the time came, she divided herself into two pieces so she would have somebody to marry. They lived a long time in that house. They prospered.

The girl fed the fish, morning and evening.

One day, she gave them a finger to eat. The next day, a long shin bone, and the next, an elbow. Little by little the little fish swam through her until there was nothing left but a pair of soft white shoes.

Then it rained again.

2. The Physician's Wife

Once there was a physician. He was attentive, his eyes were bright. He wore a white wig, a periwinkle coat; his cheeks were sunken with thought, his forehead folded in wisdom. On his fingers, he wore five fine rings. He had a wife, of whom he was fond. She also wore a white wig. They lived by a slow river full of dark weeds and leeches. His wife collected the leeches for him, in an elegant glass jar, to give to his patients. She was very fond of him. All day he would see his patients. He listened as they ran through all the tremors, flutters, spasms, sharp knocks and rustlings, bustlings, wheezings, sneezings, blowings, whistlings and snortings, each frail complainant. He had great faith in the powers of speech. He found that as they itemized the peculiarities of their pain, the pain itself seemed to lessen. The physician was fascinated. Because, you see, he had himself never felt pain. He did not know what it was. He would sit in his study, surrounded by white candles that singed the edges of his white curling wig, and write down everything that his patients had told him. He even added embellishments. When this was done, he would place the accounts carefully in a drawer in his desk, marked "confessions." His wife never looked in there. She had great respect for the sanctity of the confessional. One day, it began to rain. The river swelled. The physician woke up with a twinge in his throat, as though there was a little tear there. The rain went on falling. He was in pain at last. In great excitement, he gestured to his wife. He found he could not speak. She shook her head, perplexed. He jumped from foot to foot, he danced her around the room, he spun her down the stairs. She smiled fondly, shook her head, went off to make tea. The rain fell, danced before his eyes; nothing had ever been so beautiful. He went into his study and began to write. As he wrote he felt his body begin to curl, shrivelling like a salted leech. He wrote faster and faster, until his pen sliced and tore at the paper. The wind howled in his throat. He became so small that he could not see over the edge of his desk. So, with his remaining strength, he signed the paper with trembling hands, folded it, and dropped it in the drawer. Shrinking rapidly, he tottered and clambered into the drawer himself. He folded himself up and turned into a seed, small and black on top of a pile of papers.

When his wife came in, wet from the rain and tired from collecting leeches in the river, she wiped her shoes carefully and knocked on the study door. When no answer came, she knocked again, and when there was still no answer, she went into the drawing room and espoused the single life from that day forward. Her husband lay pea-sized on the papers of his confession and fretted. She never looked in the desk drawer. She had great respect for the sanctity of the confessional.

3. Old Ophelia

Before she was entirely carried away by the flood, she called out the litany of her long life, clutching a red handkerchief and a few flowers.

I have seen it! I have seen it! she cried over the crashing waves and the green swell, the fish, tin cans, toxic waste and infinite orange objects, all the netted, cast-up, final communications of water.

I have seen the rushed burials, the deserted suburbs and cracked streets, the old who remember the uses of words but lie about it, the crazed ownerless house pets running down alleyways—all those terrible small dogs. I have seen my husband ride by on the back of my neighbour, and both of them wore dark suits and silver crowns. My husband lost his front teeth and combed the whole city looking for them, found them clasped in the fat fist of a small boy.

How beautiful I was then, between the wars, with my slip showing.

How beautiful I was! she shrieked. I was the voice calling in the wilderness, I was the beginning of the day, the seasonal sale, the lunch special before 3:00 p.m. I have seen great rifts open in the ground, I have seen the end of writing and the poets burned in the miracles of modern architecture, I have seen the sun go down for the last time and rise again from force of habit, I have seen generations abolish themselves and men made unnecessary by obeying orders, I have churned up a dozen children and done without them in the end, and I am resigned to the new nightfall. O the days that I have seen!

And she threw the flowers and the handkerchief to a group of children standing on the bank and was carried away.

The children pocketed these treasures and wondered what the old woman had meant. Except for the rising water, everything was fine.

Girls Watch in the Mirror at Midnight for a Vision of a Future Husband

Bloody Mary, patron saint of fear, of the future,
dark lady of girls' rooms that roil
with perfume, sweat, dark hair sprouting
like fungus. Girls gathered round the mirror's light,
calling to the woman veiled, weeping tears of blood,
Bloody Mary.

And it's said if she's asked in *the right way* in *the right way* with
obedient breath, with smooth tongue, she'll show in the mirror
a man, husband, bright spark, a rescue,
a man, waiting there.

So girls, little girls, their tongues
stuttering their names, gather and wait.
Bloody Mary, Bloody Mary, Bloody Mary—

blood pumping, careful, careful,
do not watch her so closely, do not touch
the mirror, do not say her name
too loudly, Bloody Mary, patron saint of fear,
other Mary, other mother in the mirror—she'll come

forward, reach through glass, pull
you into the mirror beside her, behind her, weeping

tears of blood, and there will be no man there.

Dark Age

After Rome, a season of cloud. The roads grew over.

A huddled hungry people waited
through an empire until that winter when the river froze.
They rode over roaring and burned all the shining cities,
burned the books.

Now, in these uncertain hours the rain falls like blows,
and all eyes turn to the shore, fearful of ships and strangers,
the wolf in the wood, the face in the window.

Monks copy words by impotent candles,
hoarding memory
in hard quill strokes.

In dreams, I am visited particularly by one young monk,
small and stammering, with broken fingernails.
He transcribes with a peculiar fire,
hoping this fidelity
may save his soul.

He treads through my sleep, breaking little paths
with his chapped feet, hovering
with black quill
on the edge of waking.

The Sin Eater

These are funeral biscuits, dipped in wine, sin taken into the body, dense and dark. Lodged there in the stomach, passed through the blood, colouring the urine but never quite pissed away.

Sins are his best and dearest food, and he lives by promising salvation to others, as priests do. But he lives in the ragged fields; his breath rattles through his withered chest, his fingernails bleed frequently, and his eyes are yellow as a cat's and shine in the dark. Children cower before him, but he blesses them all the same, his fingers fluttering over their shaking pallid heads, their hair dry as straw.

He speaks Latin and a garble of nothing, he speaks the chicken bones and dirty rags the villagers throw out at the edges of town. When he dies, they will strip his flesh carefully with their little knives and they will burn his body and throw the ashes into the river that flows away from the town, and they will do this in agreement with each other so his body, buried, will not nourish any part of their crop, in case a morsel of his eaten sins were to pass their pale sanctified lips and so into their hearts. They are a fearful people, living as they do between the river and the wood, and who can blame them if they are cautious with their food.

The Witch and the Birds

She keeps them in wicker cages, pretty maidens, pretty girls, throats necklaced with feathers. They would be lost without her, she reminds them. The wood is very deep, very dark; she lives in the middle of the wood and her house is not gingerbread but terrible stone. Lost in the wood, as they were, ringed round with branches, all that fine flesh torn, the moon watching them through the trees all night. The witch now keeps them shuttered but her halls are bright, the sun shines in even in deep winter, when their poor transformed claws freeze to the perch, those claws that once were hands, those throats that once chafed against high collars. The witch is white as milk, red as blood, dark as ebony. She sits eating seeds and the youngest ones fly to her and shit on her shoulders and she feeds them seeds from her own wet small mouth. Birdsong shrieks and beats around her happy solitude and means nothing to her because, for all her cleverness, she cannot understand one single trill. But the birds all sing together, all sweetly together they sing: mother, mother, who shall bury me?

The Girl on the Road

The girl walked along the road she had a dress and shoes and a fine white loaf for when she was hungry but the tree cried to her *oh pity me pity me* and she took the loaf and broke it and hung it on the bare branches of the trees and walked on along the road and her shoes sunk deep into the ruts of the road and the wind sang in her ears and her hair was carried behind her by the hollow hard wind and she came to a boy who was thin as a tree and he cried *oh pity me pity me* so she took off her shoes and slipped them onto his sharp-boned bare feet and the girl walked shoeless along the road and her feet bled in streams of red behind her and she came to an old woman who was naked and the old woman cried *oh pity me pity me* and the girl took off her dress and put it on the old woman and the girl walked on naked down the road and the road mocked her cold nakedness and all there was for her was the wind behind her and around her and before her and the girl cried *oh pity me pity me* and the moon took pity on her and loosed a dress that fell all around her and the girl lay down on the road and slept until the wind blew thin through her and blew her away.

Family History

My grandmother says: My father
was the baker's son. They were important people
and had an indoor toilet. The only people in the village
to match them were the minister and the teacher.

She says: He wanted to be an artist, but his father
said no, and beat him round the ears and gave him
a hat and a walking stick, made him an apprentice.

When he met my mother he fell in love. She lived
in the next village. He walked a lot, bought candy for her sisters,
finally asked her parents for her hand.

Then he sold eggs, built them up and up
into a tower of cracked gold wealth. O how he made money!
First a basement apartment, then an upper floor, then a house.

The eggs lived in a cold room. We had a driver
and a maid, not much older than my oldest brother;
we four children teased her till she cried. Good years.

Then the war, all the eggs lost,
rolling down dark alleys. The driver
was shot, the maid
went to work in a factory.

After, there was nothing anywhere.

So he grew tomatoes in a field—squashed red
globes—sold them, kept a goat in the cellar.
He and the goat were good friends; when he went out
he had to go quietly or the goat
would follow him down the pockmarked Berlin street.

Then he made shingles. So things were alright, but
his storeroom burnt down one night; shingles are wood,
they catch easily.

After that, she says, I don't remember what he did. That
was a long time ago, and he was old.

Anyway, by then I was here. It's too hard
to remember everything.

Learning to Read

See this—this is the first letter of your first word.

To me, it means running. To you, something else.

This letter means flight:
a bird,

a machine, the timed exit in the middle of the night, the knock on the wall,
the broken lock.

This one is a scar, this one a fresh cut.

This one: a fall into the fire, accidental, and you screamed for hours but

really you're still a small boy.

This one at the bottom of the page is sweetness.

In the corner, rescue, and below it, history.

The last one is a door, only for you, and behind it

one more, so small you can't read it, meaning not yet.

So you take it, and pass it on.

NOTES AND ACKNOWLEDGEMENTS

Some of these poems appeared, in slightly different forms and sometimes under different titles, in *The Antigonish Review, CV2, Dandelion, Descant, Existere, The Fiddlehead, The Literary Review of Canada* and *Room*. Thanks to the editors.

Early versions of the manuscript were read with care and attention by Jessica Moore, who gave me support through the compiling and editing. Other early readers were Lea Ambros, Anna Bekerman, Simone Rosenberg and Kilby Smith-McGregor. Many, many thanks.

Thanks to another early reader, Penny Goldsmith, who asked me ten years ago if I had considered writing a collection of poetry, and then made me do it.

Thanks to my parents, David Cayley and Jutta Mason.

Thanks to everyone at Brick Books for such good care and for putting me in such good company. Particular thanks to Sue Sinclair for patient, precise attention, for fostering the strengths and seeing the pitfalls, and for urging me to look closer. Working with you was a joy.

Many of the photographs that inspired the second section of the book are in the William James Collection of the City of Toronto Archives. Thanks to the archivists.

Thanks to the Toronto Arts Council and the Ontario Arts Council for supporting me at various points while these poems were written, and to *Arc* and *Hamilton Arts and Letters,* for recommending me for support through the OAC's Writers' Reserve Program.

Thanks to Tarragon Theatre for giving me a space in which to write.

The quotation at the end of "Reading Gwendolyn MacEwen's T. E. Lawrence Poems" is from MacEwen's poem "Our Child Which Art in Heaven."

Thanks to Theatre Smith-Gilmour, whose production *GRIMM too* inspired "The Witch and the Birds" and "The Girl on the Road."

"Family History" is for my grandmother, Heidi Bechmann (1925-2011).

"Learning to Read" is for David White.

Final thanks to Lea Ambros for having every kind of faith in me, all the time (for we know how to spend the time, who cares about the weather).

Kate Cayley's poetry and short stories have appeared in literary magazines across the country. In 2011 her play *After Akhmatova* was produced by Tarragon Theatre, where she is a playwright-in-residence, and a young adult novel, *The Hangman in the Mirror*, was published by Annick Press. She is also the artistic director of Stranger Theatre and has written, directed and co-created eight plays with the company. She lives in Toronto with her partner and their two children. This is her first book of poems.